In Other Words

In Other Words

MARY MADEC

with best wishes,

Mary Madec

salmonpoetry

Published in 2010 by
Salmon Poetry
Cliffs of Moher, County Clare, Ireland
Website: www.salmonpoetry.com
Email: info@salmonpoetry.com

ISBN 978-1-907056-34-5

Cover artwork: *Quietism I, oil on canvas, by Charlotte Kelly* – *www.charlottekelly.com*
Cover design & typesetting: *Siobhán Hutson*
Printed in England by imprint*digital*.net

Salmon Poetry receives financial assistance from the Arts Council.

Acknowledgements

Acknowledgements are due to the following publications, in which some of these poems first appeared:

Crannóg, West 47, The Cúirt Annual, Revival, WOW, Boyne Berries, Poetry Ireland Review, The SHOp, The Sunday Tribune, Southward, Windows 2007, Iota, Nth Position, and *Natural Bridge*.

'Thirty Years On' was runner up in the Raftery Competition 2007, 'Bull' was runner up in the Maria Edgeworth competition 2008 and 'In Other Words' took the Hennessy XO Prize for Emerging Poetry in 2008.

Contents

Part One

Twin

The first time I dreamt
someone else was in my world,
I turned,
floating inside by a dark red light,
surprised,
by another creating tides,
against purple rib railings
arching to tunnel
the anticipatory light of early morning,
beginning of life.

The Morning I Was Born

It was snowing
the whitest tears that ever fell.

My father held his frosty breath
as he begged for petrol at a closed station,

my mother, raw, recovering
after fourteen injections of pethedine.

How she dances down the corridor
her silk kimono billowing in the icy winds,
"One for him, one for me" playing hopscotch
on the tiled floor of the nursery.

She casts the crier from the window
pink turning purple in the snow.
His waiting arms intercept, understand the division of labour,
"Pink and blue!" she cries.

She is woken by his voice,
"I'm here at last", he sighs
taking her hand, turning to see the babies,
snowflakes falling off his cap
onto their tiny faces.

Decline Your Life

Beyond the nominative case,

the vocative, a place
where you must wait for others to call you,
hear your name;

the accusative, where you stay
until the age of reason,
struggle your whole life to get beyond.

The genitive, accretions of centuries,
what you know of your ancestors
in your gestures, more solid than memories.

The dative, where you receive
a mirror,
a reflection.

The ablative, the agency you acquire
as you move through time,
the good deeds by which you shape others.

By, with, and from you
someone is starting out again
on your paradigm.

Calliope

She knows someone is parsing her body,
trying to decipher the rules by which she is put together.

She knows someone is observing her principles
of engagement as subject,

working up a theory of how
or if the head or heart rules.

She feels someone's gaze, as the morphology of her limbs,
her face is searched for some logic of expression,

even the size of her thumbs, the shape of her fingernails
her teeth set into a formula

of who she might be
as she inflects her voice.

She knows someone is secretly wondering
how she is conjugated by tense and mood

assessing the aptness of her adverbs,
her adjectives on nouns.

And she, author, oracle
desires to be the shaper of her own truth,

Poet not muse.

Part Two

Thirty Years On

If you had been preserved in a bog like Oldcroghan man,
one gesture would remain:
your thumb touching your ring finger
as your index flicks ash;

your eyes lost in some distant truth;
and out over the landscape
wisps of bog cotton
rising through sphagnum.

Jacksnipe At Evening

The *gabhairín deorach*'s dusky wings whisk against the darkness,
plaintive vowels stretched to tautness on blackthorn branches.

Black sloes whiten, soften, ripen,
smudge on the dark blue horizon.

My father leans on the pillar of an old gate,
his cigarette lights up as he inhales,

an odd car on the main road
chugs, a world away.

A Trajectory Of Grief

I set out your place
wait at six for the doorbell,
your face at the backdoor.

With the coming of night
suspended in disbelief
in the dark, I search for you.

Celestial bodies
make their habitual course
and the world goes on as before.

I imagine you living
without the heat of the sun
pale, cold beneath its shadow.

I stretch out my hand
to find yours
and rain flows down the bark

of the trees in the garden
dripping softly through
the leaves, weighing them down.

I hang onto the pendulum
between routine and ritual
to keep my centre of gravity.

The cloud forms whipped up by March
bode good. You're at peace.
Colours are brighter than before.

Earth Mother

*"I thought the earth remembered me, she took me back
so tenderly…"*
                                        MARY OLIVER

A July day:
dawn comes up through the yellow roots
of the old grass, the green stubble of the new.

Our playfields stretch out over Clew Bay,
journeys charted in faraway places until it is time
to say goodbye:

to the stones
in the stream where I built a pool
for my dolls;

to Pacadeirí where I gathered
flowers for the May procession;

to my train, no longer running
on the thick fence of the meadow;

to my fancy home in the fairy fort
on the far hill.

Croagh Patrick changing station
as I moved around
forty acres of marshy ground.

The search for goatherds
on Cnoc Mhaoill,
the nanny's milk squirted into my eyes,
our laughs echoing over the valley.

The earth here remembers me
takes me into her lap,
covers me in her soft garments,
moss and singing grass.

Her Name Was Lily

She was blonde
had blue eyes that opened and closed
and a blue dress with a lace trim.

When my aunt, on holidays from Boston
offered her to me in McGreevey's toyshop
I was as happy as the mother of a newborn.

The sun shone through the trees on the mall,
her new chewing-gum smell
warm like flesh.

I wrapped her in old baby blankets,
took her for walks
on our bumpy road.

I was only willing to leave her alone
for the joy of picking her up later
to see her blue eyes open.

One day I got too old
to reanimate her morning cold.
Couldn't pretend anymore.

When her eyes opened
they were looking at nothing,
belonged to the room, not me.

She contracted into a snapshot on the bed,
the light of the morning hitting me
hard in the eyes.

She unblinking, unmoved.

Pleasure

It all goes back to a dead rat,
his nose dripping with rain,
his eyes unreliably closed.

Blood and water flow from his side
into the silent sandpit;
mothers shout at us to keep away

as we stir his tail with a long stick,
fear its coils of disease,
and the meanness of our pleasure.

Going To The Well

The girl going to the well is my sister,
doing as she is told,
drawing water from the spring
at the bottom of Michael Joe's field.

She is afraid of the neighbours she might meet
asking, "How's your father today?"
She crosses over the gate and hurries in case
the cows become curious.

When she returns, the kettle goes on,
new rounds of tea and silences.
Later, buckets of tears,
hands plunged into holy water, to bless our dead father.

The house we shared with him fills with people
we hardly know.
I could hear someone say,
"Is that the youngest one
we saw on the way to the well for water?"

Out Walking

He waltzed with him down the country road
trying to stop him from falling as he got used to walking
without the Zimmer-frame.

Glad it was not a street
where people would see
him taking his Dad for a walk.

Knew that if other children could tease
they would
except he was the Master's son.

His shame: to wish his father like other men
able-bodied leading the conversation
instead of failing to follow.

He's not quite an alien, he remembers his name
but it doesn't feel like the same Dad
he'd known, who demanded

His hair cut
Respect for his elders
Application at school

He made the rules a year ago.
Now his son cajoles him
up the hill,

can just about take the weight
of keeping him straight on the road.

Puppet On A String

I never saw your small room,
only the contractions of the walls at home,
when you were packed away.
All on the list into your hard suitcase –
I wondered whether you liked wearing
the dressing gown and slippers.

I needed the light on to sleep. Home
was not the same without you, especially at bedtime.
As days went into weeks, each night
we all knelt down and joined our hands:
My mother led the *God bless Andy*
up in Dublin, far away from home.

I couldn't really understand why you had to go.
I couldn't understand what you did all day.
When it came to mealtimes, did you get mashed potato
and homemade bread? And when you were lonely at night,
rocking from side to side, did you look at the moon?
I hoped you were at home in the sea of tranquillity.

They got on the phone and told us you cried
for three days. I think they all thought you weren't able
to produce real tears. Though you were homesick, I was glad
when they said you could sing *Puppet on a String*
so I sang the words for you: *I wonder if some day that you'll say that*
*Someday that you'll say…*you want to come home.

On our first visit to Stewart's Hospital
it took a long search to find you. I spotted you
behind the chicken-wire fence at the bottom of the play yard.
My parents said later you were pale and thin.
No roses in your cheeks. You were making wipers
with your hands, barely glanced at us
but I noted the eyelid flicker; your gladness we had come.

When we left, I said, "We can't leave him alone,
it's too big here, he knows no-one."
If I could have said, "There's only half of me at home
since he went away", I would. Instead I looked through
the windows of the train at the world unravelling
spelling out two words on the foggy glass: *Andy Home.*

When They Told Me About My Brother

I ran like the Ugly Duckling to a silent lake seeking cover
from the wild wet winds coming in on the shiver of the dawn;

I tried to construct the new word, sounded out what I heard, "*a tistic*"
over the drumlins of home; low-lying clouds pressing in on my throat.

I wondered about what they said, about *how* my brother was *artistic*,
was wounded already that no-one would like my pictures anymore.
I didn't know that "r" could colour a vowel;

when it lost its colour, it fell into a dropped chin,
an "r-lessness" that made it difficult to be a twin
but taught me to listen for the double-cross words.

Beyond Words

You find words confusing,
never use them,
yet, have to decode them,
make vain attempts to unload
double-entendres, sous-entendus.

From what I know
you might be better off without them,
their weary endless possibilities.

Their limits on the page.

How you'll draw a blank
when you glance over this note.

Unless I translate
with warm intonations.

Then, your face breaks into a smile,
as if you read between the lines.

Might Be Worth Knowing

after Sujata Bhatt

Speaking of Van Gogh, looking perhaps at his swirls
of midnight light over St Rémy or Arles
that he believed stars are the souls of dead poets,

that he knew how to wield a pen, wrote eight hundred letters
to his younger brother Théo, wheedling lifelines
on which he propped his mind.

Hypergraphia, we are told
linked to his temporal lobe epilepsy,
aggravated by Absinthe, arguments, bipolar disorder.

We do not know when he imploded
and painted frenetically at St. Paul's
whether he was attempting to understand

his disintegrating mind or the spiritual essence of man
and nature. Of where he fitted in the vast expanse
of the universe.

His life stretched like a canvas,
from the pulpit of a preacher in the Borinage
to the bedposts of a prostitute in the Hague.

A tightrope, which might have brought him to state
that refraining from sex was good for art.
So he grew celibate, like a single-minded monk

became intimate with every pixel of colour
on his palette, and was drawn in,
swirled into the vortex of his inner life.

His favourite plant not the sunflower
but ivy, which connected things,
connected him to Théo

who listened and believed in him
accepted his strange sibling
knew above all

that without his fragile brother
there could be no *Potato Eaters*, *Sunflowers*,
Almond Blossoms, *Fields of Provence*...

and no night skies with their swirling light.
Théo grieved in the knowledge that to become a poet
you have to die.

Part Three

Declaration

I redden from the root up through my shoes
into my thighs.

Heat rises through my skin into my cheeks,
the pulse of its force in my head,

my unsophisticated eyes made small
by the change in perspective.

You might have seen my red thoughts
when you called love a chemical reaction of the blood,

said something about a body
forgetting gravity.

But I knew what you were telling me,
as you lifted your head from my lap, struggled for words

to express that you loved her
but wouldn't stop her from going for a white sari and
celibacy in Calcutta.

Your tears cooled the rawness of exposure
but put salt in the wound of not being chosen.

Breakers

I feel your distance from me,
cold flowing over my feet in the damp sand.

The mist, the seagulls,
the still air carry memories.

I am inclined to your body,
a shape in the murk,
lying in tangles of washed-up wrack.

The ebb of our tide, a cyclic fall.
In a world without light, the Sun and Moon
no longer attract,

our faces opaque, your once-warm hands ice,
your strong arms sticks in the sea.

I cannot help looking back, footprints filling
with salt water. Purple light
on the backwash.

Preparing Sunday Dinner

She has lost weight and is wondering how long
it will take for the pounds to creep back on.
It's partly the shock of her new size,
makes her body seem like one she doesn't deserve.
When men show interest, it sends her
scurrying in panic, after years of telling herself,
that it's her mind they'd like.
Emerging from her wads of protection
she imagines the Emperor when he realised
he had no clothes. Maybe not him.

Maybe the chicken she is preparing for dinner,
cutting off the dense white fat near the Pope's Nose
and sprinkling it with aphrodisiac pepper, salt.
She wonders how she got to think of herself like this.
She puts the deadweight of the chicken in the oven
afraid to feel her limbs.
Was it something subliminal or plain grief,
made her body seem not hers?
She thinks how cruelly she has carried out
someone else's mission of mean words,
sorts the forks and knives which clang flat on the table,
prongs and blades upwards.

Ariadne

So, you saved Theseus
with a single thread

and you want me to forget
it was a leash.

Admit, your motives were not as pure
as your name suggests,

your thread red and resilient,
a lusting artery,

a bulging carotid, Ariadne,
a snake pulsing under silk.

It came from your own web.
At the heart of it: desires for yourself.

Hardly a surprise that you could not trust your man
to come back, no matter how hard you tried.

Was it lack of confidence, Ariadne
in yourself, shame for your plan?

In the end, you gave too much,
unravelled to your centre.

It wasn't wise Ariadne.
It's only yours if it comes back.

You know this, you retort,
in the retrospect of black sails.

Nature forgives outcomes we didn't plan.
History remembers you without a man,

forgets you died pregnant. Remembers only
that you gave Theseus a way out.

And he left you.

Part Four

The Summer

You worked on the aerospace building
in Trafalgar Square,
I'd pick you up for lunch,
to the amusement of the workmen whistling –
they'd never guess – at your wife.

We'd sit on the steps,
share sandwiches with the pigeons,
our laughter lines from Beckett,
something about legs astride a grave,
too vague then to worry about.

We'd run for a takeaway coffee on the corner,
check out *Marks and Spencer's*
for air-conditioning
as the July sun rolled heavily
across the city.

In the evening we'd meet for the train
Minding the Gap at Elephant and Castle,
analyzing all the new ways of using
the same language,
laughing at the workmates who thought you were
A *fucking Paddy*,
couldn't hear your French accent.

We violated their rules,
doing what was easy to do, then,
reviewing with slick certitude
the world around us.

Under The Maybush

I smell the air, the hawthorn in the breeze.
May is the nicest month of all, you say,
our memories stir confetti from the trees.

The drifts of white are weighing down the leaves.
May is always great for us, you say.
I smell the air, the hawthorn in the breeze.

Or is it your fragrant body, now at ease,
stretched on the soft-grass where you lie at play.
Our memories stir confetti from the trees.

The flower-fall will make our love increase,
I feel the softness of this summer's day.
I smell the air, the hawthorn in the breeze.

The perfume's faint, and tender slow release –
Come, come to me my love without delay.
Our memories stir confetti from the trees.

The sweetness of your breath will never cease
To take me by surprise, I say.
You put your mouth on mine, you start to tease.
I smell the air, the hawthorn in the breeze.

Yarn

"I spin this yarn from the stuff of yearning"
THE WIFE'S LAMENT trans. Damian Love

In the evening exhausted, I do chores on autopilot,
gather gloom, as I sort the forks, knives, spoons
from the dishwasher, gather up the dirty clothes
from the bathroom after the children shower,
make note of changes in the morning rota,
attach to the fridge.

I google the Wife of the *Exeter Book* out of time,
see her struggle with loving a man,
it's the same story over and over. Busy-body relations
coming between them. She wants to know what pains him.
but the hills are watching, the hedgerows closing in;
alone, she recites her mantra of wise dispositions.

You come through the door, after your day at work
too tired for words, words unable to bridge the gaps
of the day. So you stay in silence,
hard and bitter enough to sprout a spiked plank of wood
in the middle of our bed,
yet strong enough to make a boat to ride the water between our islands.

What the Wife longed for in the geography of love:
promontories, our touching fingers,
harbours, the curved cavities of our arching hips,
hills and hollows, the rises and dips of our skeletons,
soft moss, our skin.

By morning the old landscape forming, man-made edifices looming
as we move apart to our daily routines,
pick out our paths on the low tide we made last night
to the earth-caves on our islands where we spin stories
through the traffic of the day, rehearse conversations for dinner
or mantras to comfort us when one of us is away.

How Do I Love Thee?

After Elizabeth Barrett Browning

Let me count the ways.
I love your bones, how they thrive
on gravity and the hardness of the road;
your muscles' soft resilience, how they contain you
and me when I am with you;
your fat, how it cushions vulnerable bits,
gives you something to fall back on
and me something to hold.
I love the primal comfort coming
through what one might call a soul,
your life, the light that comes across your face
now in focus and familiar –
and your voice, always with the right timbre,
as you say o miracle of miracles, my name.

By Name

One day I heard my name
as a solace, an index of intimacy, a claim,
which you made on me (and which I was glad you were making).

When you moved your mouth to form the two syllables,
I heard a call to come forward,
be myself.   (Or the self you know and love).

Somehow in answering to the way you made it sound,
I became a person unique in all the world,
no longer in the crowd, no longer alone.

Now And Always

We are the warp and weft
of a garment greater than ourselves,
the pattern of its vibrant threads
in retrospect, interesting, deft.

When you took my hand
we wove the background thread,
strong, resistant, yet soft to caress,
in it the narrative of the living and the dead.

We learned to pick up stitches, mend wounds,
to see defects as proof of what we had overcome,
our own mouths finding the way
to make new threads where worms grew,

our fingers interlocked
to carry our children
or released to tease out patiently knots
and runs, change them to ladders, slubs,

our minds playing threads
following the fairisle to get the picture,
our hearts a cocoon of dreams,
the junction a permanent suture.

So here we stand aware of frays
and fringes we had not chosen.
A more regal fabric
we could not have woven.

With these robes, my love
I comfort you, I wrap your days
in the scent of our memories
and your nights in unfathomable tenderness

Part Five

At Sea

At first she is afraid of her body,
overwhelmed by its redeployment
of good energy against her,

producing lumps
in breast, axilla, bone,
deposits from a violent inner storm.

She tries to make friends,
goes to the sea where she learns peace
on the shores of her childhood:

winter nights, silent, accomplished,
where fears are tamed,
reasoned, put into perspective,

the Plough searched out, the Evening Star
still promises full light
in this darkness,
where no one can reach her.

An inner grace comes in waves,
covering the indignity of hypostatic pneumonia,
detaching catheters.

Pope Has Breast Cancer

A source from the Vatican revealed last night
that Her Holiness Pope Christina the first has been diagnosed
at the Gemelli Clinic,
with a tumour in the inner quadrant of her left breast.

Her doctors assured the Faithful that her chances are good,
words whispered were *stage one* and *contained*.
They were also keen to mention that she is praying
to her favourite saint, Agatha.

It is snowing in Rome.
The pigeons are falling down in St. Peter's Square.
There is one question on the blue lips of her cardinals:
Will she be able to make her *urbe et orbi* this year?

The women of the world are looking for consoling words,
breasts heavy with feeding,
sagging from gravity,
prostheses in loco,
all praying this night
for the Holy Mother and Father Church.

My Doctor Rocks

Coming to visit me after
bilateral resection of tangled parts of my insides.

I tell him his tie is a perfect match
for his eyes
– Must be the morphine shots –
I want to tell him how wonderful he is
to have undertaken this,
saved me.

Two years later I pick up the phone
boldly ring him to say
I had the baby against all the odds.

I can feel his smile over the line
then, mild dismay.
He's already revising his paper on,
The complications of multiple adhesions in young females.

Birth Announcement

Just as we enter the cloister a young man comes towards me,
signs at the sky
and my abdomen,

pirouettes, rocks a baby, kneels:
I am Mary, he is the angel
joy in his face.

Then, he disappears into the crowd,
leaves me speechless,
sheltering among the capitals from a cloudburst.

The Clintons Are In Ireland

I am in a hospital bed,
balancing drain and drip, as I raise my head
to see – above me – Hilary Rodham Clinton,
presented to *mná na hÉireann* –
and Finola Bruton decry
the neglect of fatherless boys.

The sway of the curtains in the breeze,
heat of the room,
nothing fully understood,
Van Gogh's sunflowers explode
on the opposite wall.

When my eyes open again,
my motherless baby boy
surveying tubes, distant, afraid
to cuddle up,
the ladder of my ribcage broken,
his pillow torn open.

About Happiness

There is always the flip side that ensures
none of us can confidently say we have a happy life.

For, as we are wallowing in love,
somewhere we are weeping in the future,
lonely, separated, lost.

As we are thanking God for our health
some cancer may be establishing itself:

Our broad teeth-white smile
easily tautened by a sudden
change of circumstance, inclusion of other facts.

Yet, we stand over our graves and losses,
insist that we are happy,

for the gifts given and taken away;
we find even exhilaration in our grief
as we connect themes in our lives,

concede the necessity of pain.
as we sew the seams across the years.

Needles bleed in our hands
as we stitch the bandages on our lives,
weave happiness from them,

into a garment that looks plush on the outside,
one Job wore.

Demeter's Plea

*"I'm no more your mother
Than the cloud that distills a mirror to reflect its own slow
Effacement at the wind's hand."*

"Morning Song" by SYLVIA PLATH

You saw me avert my eyes, Persephone,
from the cave-pool dark and trembling
from the wind, my face turning
into a steely mask with a shiny smile that you feared.
I became hard from doing without you, Persephone.
Now I am vulnerable as glass,
my eyes opaque marbles of ice.
I know you were hoping that one day
you would see into the darkness of them.
You will have to wait to peel potsherds
from this red clay among the votives on the ground.

I was aggrieved by your nuptials, Persephone,
you, more like Aphrodite than my daughter,
a nubile bride of the underworld, no longer my child.
And yet, you were, are, me.
So I hold back from you, afraid of the angry threads
I found in Hera's robe.
I still pray to her for sky and sun,
for your return, Persephone.
I raise my head to water flowing down my face,
look down to the sound of my feet stomping frozen ground.
Hungry birds linger for a trickle.

Could we let winter end so they could sing?
Endure, my daughter, the pain of thaw?
I am breathing into the frosty mouth of the Grotta Caruso
Persephone, come out!

Miracle At Lourdes

She will give you a stone, blue lace agate, and though
it is hard and shiny, it will pulse in your hand,
turn warm.

You will fall to your knees in the wet earth,
her voice will sound soft in the damp air.
The one who gave birth to you will spread out her cloak,
gaze upon you without tears in her eyes.

The fish will jump in the Gave,
the grass on the hills in Bartrès will sing.

You will know the secret of polished rock,
in the black womb of the Grotto:
Jags and splinters,
sculpted by delicate fingers,
to carry
            the deep tributaries
                        on the long dark river
of mother and daughter.

Bath

She lies immobile as a crocodile,
the candle casting shadows in the darkness.
When she moves her limbs
a tide breaks the silence,
bubbles disappearing
in intricate puffs over her skin,
glistening in the candlelight.

When they call her
she cannot bring herself to utter a word.
She hears their frantic searching of the house,
Mammy where are you?

When they finally find her watery hideout
in the avocado bath of their seventies home,
they walk away angry at her,
a little afraid that she put the lights out,
Weird, they say.

When they leave she turns over in the bath
to warm her underside,
wonders what besides the darkness possessed her.

Bull

Maeve's a legend
Runs around in her chariot 4x4
Picks up the kids from school
Each one of seven in training
To outdo the fellas next door
A competitive parent type

A woman to best any man
Wife and business woman of the year
She answers clients' calls yet
Has a wash in, dinner in the oven
An invoice filled, iron in hand
The kettle on

When there's strife
She knows to take the bull
By the horns
Woe betide the man
Who raises himself to her size
Her old boyfriends drop to the floor
As she settles old scores

When she goes out she's a tonic
And when she croons
Drink to me only with thine eyes
Her husband teases her
That the boss during the day
Is not the boss at night
Even if she runs out of biofuel
She revs up to put manners on him
It's the *Táin Bó Culaigne* all over again

She Tells Herself

Every woman should carry herself well,
be proud of her history,
which she should, nonetheless, carry lightly.
All one need know is that she got through.

She should carry dreams
the ones she has had over tea in the city,
looking disconsolate through glass
at the passage of humanity.

She should carry through
on all her promises,
especially ones she made to herself
after betrayal.

There's so much she will carry
against her will,
marks of lovers' indelicacies,
weight but not in conversations,

the mesh of insights
and memories
pulled over wounds
that do not heal.

As life goes on she will do well
to carry a smile
and a pen and paper
to record the contradictions.

She will be carried away
on these pillars of sanity,
and when all is useless and impossible
this is what will give her the courage

to carry on.

Part Six

Cartographer

You knew that country when you were young
as you leaned against the window sill
your breasts pert against a slice of moon
sore in the chill. The populations of that country
were in the curtains at nightfall, the wallpaper in the half-light,
the two bar-heater, alive with towns.

You walked through it, holding back
on banks of country lanes from dark silhouettes,
and when it was winter and that country stood still
you felt surreal watching *Star Trek*
knowing it had no horizon.   So you went outside
the backdoor and the sky fell, pressed you into
the vinyl floor sweating from winter.

That country you knew when you were young
you could never give directions to, its longitude and latitude
the breadth and depth of your memory;
you might have said "come *here*" if you were able,
but you stayed *there*, your feet stuck
in mud, the suck of your wellies pressing you into the earth.
The boundary, the bedroom door, closed at night,
so you lost your bearings; and the exit you sought
when you sleep-walked, always the wardrobe.
So when you played house, you marked it out
with open-plan rooms, made it roofless, with surround light.

You grew up in that country
somehow all of your making.
And one day you no longer belonged to it.
It belonged to you and you were glad
it was far away.

Good Old Days

On a cold winter's evening,
when Galway was a village
and the streets closed in against the grey
pigeons, the grey of coming dark,
televisions announced tea,
the daily news of unemployment figures;
Tears on Levi's,
later, *Sally O'Brien and the way she might look at you*
Tourists looking for *Harp*.

On a quick walk to alleviate tedium
you spot on a drapery window in Abbeygate Street
an ad for "terminal underwear,"
someone spelling out your quiet life of desperation;
and on a glass door in the Cornstore
an A4 sheet with an invitation to learn a, "Marital Art."

Your mind snaps
into pieces of words
that will not pronounce themselves,
slide on a single sound
to unease and loneliness.

In the struggle of all your inner conversations
you talk to walls. There is nothing warm about concrete.
Even the tea-shops are closed. The night falls
heavy on your shoulders as you go through your front door,
shake off the evening.

Road Sign

As I drive down Taylor's Hill
on a gloomy summer afternoon,
a cloud of rain pushing down the bonnet
like a sulking friend,
in the distance I see roadworks,
a man alternating a large lollipop stick
to signal STOP or GO.

When I get up close he bows and smiles,
shows me RED but instead of feeling annoyed
at having to wait, I feel grateful
for his white teeth gleaming,
his face beaming in the thunder sky of July.

Then I notice his skin and his Reynaldo cap,
muse that perhaps he is relieved
to be away from the forty degrees in Rio de Janeiro.

I feel like I am Mary Tyler Moore or Rhoda
and he is Carlton my doorman,
somehow *turning the world on with his smile.*
He's taking on a mission to cheer up *a nothing day*:
Galway strung out by a European monsoon.
He is offering a few moments of meditation,
this high priest of the road.

As he flicks the roadsign to GREEN
I am infused with the mañana feeling;
and even as I run around this city all GO
I know something happened at the STOP today.

As I pull away I feel his benediction fall,
his obsidian eyes under his peaked cap
satisfied by his having saved another soul
with his crook and staff.
I am sure I hear him singing,
You're going to make it after all.

Journey To The New World

We take the van from JFK to Philadelphia
conjure up *King of Prussia*, struggle to see a place,
imagine some great monarch spreading out his cloak.

When we arrive to the warm welcome of our host
we wonder if this is really the king under guise,
who brings father, mother and child to *Banjo* town.

We climb the stairs
after the *Wildcats* score the winning basket,
all these new names rolling in our heads

and only the ball of the winter moon familiar
bouncing through a window without curtains.
We fall back on the soft pillows,

our ancestors who made their way
to the new world before us
caught in a prayer, the angels on our bedposts.

Does God Really Exist?

You ask,
or is it an idea people
came up with?
closing your eyes to say
your night prayers
in a strange room in Merton Drive.

The question settles like dust
on the trinket box left behind
by an old woman:
her prayerbook,
cards of favourite saints,
petitions.

> The answer remains insufficient,
> even when sleep overtakes,
> and the streetlights peep
> through the curtains.

> You leave me grappling:
> the stillness of the room,
> the trust of closing eyes.

In Other Words

I'd like to gloss your post-modern grin
with a labio-dental fricative to begin.
Then, a bilabial plosive.

God knows what would come out, if I started to use
my west-of-the-Shannon round vowels,
which you are colonising.

As you purse your lips to front yours,
I notice that it goes very well with your chic-about-town suit.
You speak foreign D4 to the men in my parts,
who respect sibilants that don't make a difference.
Know that SHTOP is surprise, not a rural marker
separating them from the wise fellas
up at the University.
Or a noun,
something they would do to sort out
a poseur like you.

You flex your intellectual biceps
obsessed, not only by your manhood
but by the kind of man you are.
The genre, an obtrusive voice,
your life, a metafiction,
a revised identity.

Now, your grandmother, a professional woman
who walked to school from May to October
in her bare feet
is unsure about her story.
It is not one of the images you are staying with today.
Your voice echoes in the 1970's box architecture
of the new Irish University,
hollow as Plato's Cave.

The sign of the times no more than
the minute's silence for Guinness,
for Irish before the singing of the national anthem.

The men in my parts still check the sky for the weather,
are ensconced in a world that loves them,
will turn up at the funeral,
pay respects to one of the best.
You wish your words still had meaning like theirs.
It's what you left behind,
men pulling their wellies up over wool socks to go out on the land,
while you lace up your expensive trainers
to jog on an asphalt running track.

You can hear the chortling of a bird
coaxing you back to your senses.
It would be too much like innocence
to know whether it is a lark in the morning,
a sparrow chattering, or a robin claiming territory.
You put up the volume, adjust your earphones,
check the zapper for the electric gate is in your pocket,
home is only a block away.

Bridge Over

"A voice comes to one in the dark. Imagine"
Company Samuel Beckett

You set yourself astride a grave,
to find the measure of your existence
against two unknowns,

the world after and the world before;
and patiently explore paths
from one to the other, a breath on the water,

a bum eating radishes or garlic
out of a paper bag on the sidewalk,
a critic wending his way from TCD,

all that you noticed on the journey,
the knowledge you gleaned of the other side
on your tightrope of extremes.

You are laid down in the city
that this town has become,
a cut above;

you stretch in steel pylons on mathematical equations
over the perturbed Liffey,
which you are happy to gaze into,

elated in the eye of the storm;
a harp that once
found words in the wind is now a prophetic lyre,

the symbol of Irishness,
and the pun on pulling strings
an extended metaphor.

You came all the way from Rotterdam
on a barge,
from there to here,

to Dublin, a spot on the Universe,
where visitors will stop
to do you homage –

not by sitting on a canal bank seat
but by standing in the insecure middle,
sur le pont

straddling past and future,
the timeline of their existence,
with no starting point, no end,

wondering if they should turn back
for something now forgotten
or forward for something yet unknown,

dashing in its multiple lanes
insanely pursuing
multiple destinations.

I stand and wait
for the moment I will know
I'll go on, when I can't go on,

why my legs don't move
when someone says *Let's go.*
Bridges prolong the dilemma.

Perhaps it should have been a roundabout,
un rond point anglais
but no, on balance, it is better this way,

Attishue, attishue we all fall down

Part Seven

Sea-Girls

Palindrome collage for T.S. Eliot

Some men interpret nine memos
Was it Eliot's toilet I saw?
Kay, a red nude peeped under a yak
In the room where the women come and go
(Talking of Michelangelo)
We few drawn inward
Til human voices wake us
And we drown

Do geese see God?
Under the brown fog
Of a winter dawn
Ah, Satan sees Natasha!
Satan, oscillate my metallic sonatas!

Madam, in Eden, I'm Adam
I am not Prince Hamlet
Nor was meant to be
God saw I was dog (tired)
Oozy rat in a sanitary zoo
Eyes I dare not meet in dreams
Good night ladies, good night

Don't nod

These fragments I have shored against my ruins
Pull up, Maria, we're here, wave, pull up
Was it felt I had a hit left, I saw

In the chambers of the sea
Darkness cover daylight

Washerwoman

(after Paul Camille Gigou, French artist 1834–1871)

The washerwoman stood over the muddy pond,
stirred the brown viscous water with a long stick,

stirred and prodded all the old clothes she had ever worn,
as they moved in awkward circles, their colours hardly distinguishable.

The washerwoman stood over them,
looked carefully at the piles coming up

above the surface, tired now from the force of pushing and shoving
and sorting what was not black and white at all,

wishing only to wring them out and let them dry in the sun,
dreaming – this is what she held to – of the tidy piles when ironing was done

But for now, her red-knuckled hands clasped the long stick,
bravely started to stir and prod, push and shove and sort again,

eye to the weather
heart to the sun.

I Am The Woman Who Took The Veil

Who in the year of our Lord
nineteen forty two, at the age of sixteen
my mother weeping at the door
my father unable to say goodbye
entered the Presentation Convent in Galway

who made the best of hard times
a way to be educated through vows
left the rudeness of country life for parlours
haggards for manicured gardens
who wept though for my mother's flowers at the south gable

who tried to bring all at home
up in the world
one rung at a time
cajoling, advising, keeping in touch

who could not know touch
only the feel of a wimple
gabardine, cotton, winter wool

who was tortured by loneliness
sacrificed, sacrificed
could not go home
to bury a mother or friend
had to wait for reports of how it all happened
imagine the scenes

who worked by day at school
who didn't like punishment
believed in *mol an óige*
my mother's mantra in my ears

who did the Legion of Mary visitation
emptied slops in Shantalla for the infirm
like mother and father at home
whom I could not visit
the rules said no

who visited the home place
After Vatican 2
the old kitchen strange and new
echoing the absence of my father and mother
my brother and wife
trying to understand how a cage of manners
held tears back

who had it hard
measured pain all the same as something good
suspected the soft life
knew how easy it was to substitute
self pity for love

who looks to the young
to tell my story
though I am a woman of my time
tired now, ready to go
a lone survivor in my convent home

who will persevere to the end
believing that with the help of God
and his holy mother
it will all make sense

who will leave no-one weeping
over my tidy grave in the garden by the canal
only a heron rising from the silence on a winter's day
a robin stopping to check the disturbed clay
long shadows in the glasshouse
my cuttings lined up on the south wall

We Are Her Still Life

The chair on which she sits,
the perching of her buttocks,
a measure of her place in conversation.

The table on which she puts her elbows, when alone,
events indented,

the old armchair,
in which she sees her dad,
her late mother, fixing flowers.

Their lost molecules
hover in our wood and glass.

The warmth of her body presses in against us,
relieves skirmishes with salty water,
cups of tea.

Nursing Home

Into that hole I went,
there was nothing to discuss in the end,

waiting for breakfast from a trolley, cold eggs and white bread,
insipid tea from a communal pot,

by golly I won't have that, I thought
but I did,

instead of my own brown bread, freshly squeezed juice,
and at the weekend Shaw's rashers and Clonakilty pud,

I might have had a small appetite
but I loved my food.

My clothes labelled with my name, chosen for ease of washing,
mixed up in their untidy press with the clothes of everyone else,

my whites grey from a colour run,
my favourite wool cardigan shrunk

bringing me down to size remembering what I left behind,
my reserve of cotton lace panties neatly folded in the drawer.

I could always look forward to putting them on
no matter how long it took me to get dressed.

The woman across from me raves, cries to God to take her.
I look at my feet and wish my nails were painted for summer sandals.

The vacuum whirrs me into naps I never remember taking.
Sometimes when I'm waking I don't know where I am.

They have put me to bed in flannelette
I dream of my husband's body close to mine.

The walnut and lacewood boat, our sixty-year old bed
all set to go into the deep where he waits for me.

I sink in, remembering ourselves alone.
The scattering of quilt,

skin on skin, bone on bone.

March

The month of raw,
fingers and thoughts.
crueler than April.

Even when the edge of the wind
which swings through the limbs
of every living thing is softened by daffodils,

it remains the month of cold promises.
The teeth of a smile in the sap.

And March whipped you away,
cries still in the doorway of January,
where they said, "terminal."

Even now its hinges swing and creak,
speak your name, tease
as if you could come back.

The wind pretends to be a breeze undoing your hair,
your nightdress peeling away,

your brush full of hairs lying idle now,
the dreams of your dressing table,
your creams and perfumes cast aside.

And outside the daffodils and the wind again
getting in through the timberframe.

The Pilot's Wife

She came down
on the side that her mother had known.

Nothing remained in the wreckage
but her hand

and the nine bracelets she wore
for each child.

At home on the cheminée
her Christmas cards stacked,

ready for posting
ahead of time.

Her husband recalled
the cadence of her voice

when she said farewell,
some intimation that he didn't understand,

wondered if she understood what made her hesitate,
then say his name as she went through the gate?

A flight in winter across Alsace-Lorraine
snowflakes covering over the portholes.

When her daughter walked through the woods
where the plane crashed
she could hear her mother's voice
rebounding on the trees.

She imagined her hand
with its bracelets in the snow,
the red ink of destiny spilling out
through her fingernails,
when she came down.

Eve

This is my body:
the contours of my limbs
my shape on the world;
the narrative of my skin
a record, which, one day, will be lost in clay.

At first a silk border,
now, it is toughened, frayed,
grey from withdrawing blood,
and the air coming up from within
catches in the pulp of my neck.
My eyes strain, confused by the know-all who told me
I was naked, tempts me to despise my skin.

I too was once a baby
stretching up, to inspect my hands, my toes,
until I grew old enough to see
the message that slid over me,
that said, "Close your little hands,
it is better if you close your hands and pray,
for the path you will take
and for what you will come to know."

I grew fat, I grew thin,
like a sad accordion,
working to make a tune
from minor notes,
the ears of the trees waiting.

I never saw how my eyes looked
in the depths of the well at which I drew,
only the dark shadow trembling on the the waters,
a reflection I dared not decipher,
the shape of desire on its surface.

I gathered my history in the folds of my flesh:
once the cells of my distressed breast became receptors for disease;
once the cells of my thighs grew purple, oblong in the cold;
once it rained off my fingers.

The shell of me hardened to a shelter
to protect a soft and frightened centre;
an epiglottis on sentry, ready to make flesh a word,
knowing that desire is not lust
just longing prior to utterance.
Silk of spring leaves as Adam speaks,
"This is my body, fragile and mortal,
I give it to you."

This touch, the weight of a summer's breeze on a meadow,
the sudden heat of sun on ripe fruit.
At this distance you dilate my pupils.
My palms rise in an embrace
to bring the beauty outside in.
Your out breath is resuscitative
but this is a rhythm which could unhinge the world.

Where was original sin?
My memories now sit like
Lady Pinks on a south-facing window,
There is a truth inside me
I will stand by;
The language from the summit
will be body,

a prayer. My apprentice fingers
trace their way back through the labyrinth of years
into the plump span of my first hand
to bless my life.

When I Am No Longer Young

I pray that I can still stand straight,
that no disease contorts my spine

so that when you come to visit,
I can look you in the eye.

And when you look at me, you see an orange,
not a prune, an old lady with stippled interesting skin.

I pray you will not spare me
the outrageous thoughts of your generation

and that my arsenal to rebut
remains intact.

I pray for a long life
but not to outlive my tribe.

When I die, I pray that it is midwinter
so I can go unobtrusively into the cold

and when you feel sad for me
the world will respect your grief.

By the time summer comes
you will have warm and happy memories.

Last Rites

We go from room to room
to say our goodbyes and thankyous.

My son stops at the shrine of his childhood
and listens for echoes of bedtime stories
and voices he gave Action Men and Transformers.

We go to the main bedroom where family was
an overcrowded bed in the middle of the night
and when there were four and one fell out

he went instead to the box room,
slept among books and notes
grateful for rest.

The kitchen and garden, we bless,
a marketplace of exchange
between us and the world;

we thank it for its measure,
and for contracting in on us
when the world went out;

we implore that the neighbour stops snoring,
and that the man in the house which overlooks ours
will avert his eagle eye;

that the feral cats scaling the walls
of the garden
will stop raiding bins and caterwauling.

When we close the door and drive away
we have already given back the space,
the naked walls quiet and indifferent,

ready for someone else to adorn.
Yet, something niggles, what if the house misses us,
if the walls are heavy and sad, stultified by our absence.

Perspective

It's a mathematical formula of sorts
that all your loves
run parallel.
Until you look back
find they converge
like traintracks in the distance,

you the epicentre
of their vanishing point.

About the Author

MARY MADEC was born and raised in the west of Ireland. She received her early education at NUI, Galway, obtaining her B.A. in French and English, and her M.A in Old English; in 2002 she received her doctorate in Linguistics from the University of Pennsylvania, USA. She has taught courses for NUI, Galway, UPenn, and Open University and is currently Director of the Villanova Study Abroad  Program in Galway. She has received awards and accolades for her work in the Raftery Competition 2007, the WINDOWS Showcase and Anthology 2007 and the Maria Edgeworth Competition 2008. In April 2008 she was also the recipient of the Hennessy XO Award for Emerging Poetry. With her husband Claude Madec of the LIFE programme (Brothers of Charity Services) she started up a community-writing project, *Away with Words*, now in its third year.